Nothing Happened Last Night

poems by

Karen Morris

Finishing Line Press
Georgetown, Kentucky

Nothing Happened
Last Night

ACKNOWLEDGMENTS

Women's Studies Quarterly: Rorschach
NY Quarterly Magazine: Nothing Happened Last Night
Writers Resist: Duende and The Great Matter of Life-and-Death
CHIRON review: Hassam mapped out the world on the café tabletop
SWWIM Everyday: You Are So Confucius, Eastern Alternatives to AA;
     "Alpha-Bait,"
CATACLYSM and Other Arrangements (Three Stones Press, PA, 2014)

Publisher: Leah Huete de Maines
Editor: Christen Kincaid
Cover Art: *Sally Skips School* by Jerry Moriarty
Author Photo: Seiso Paul Cooper
Cover Design: Elizabeth Maines McCleavy

Order online: www.finishinglinepress.com
        also available on amazon.com

Author inquiries and mail orders:
Finishing Line Press
PO Box 1626
Georgetown, Kentucky 40324
USA

Contents

Before Now and After

Lately I'm uneasy about 'the guys,' the architects
of history, conjurors of legacies, like those unlicked
Spanish Stamps, still traveling, that are become,

as John Donne wrote in *Elegies*, allegiances
pledged upon spurious hearts, daily churning out
God, fake news, and guns. Until said Now,

I've been as fortunate as any gorilla. After waking,
opening my eyes, I think for fifteen minutes.
Don't shit where I eat. Who wouldn't want

to be free of picking history's lice, flicking
its fleas? Then, I ask myself,
Do you want to get up, Now?
   Do you want to bathe, Now? Or later?
     Would you like coffee, Now? Or Tea?

Everyone wants something from me, Now.
   Come here, Now! You can't do that, Now.
    Do it, Now! Give it to me,
      Now! I want you, Now!

People under pressure don't work well together.
Where we place our hands, in and out of fantasies,
matters. Use your own head, hands, and feet.

Quick-quick. Time passes freely. Ignorance
is anonymous. Suffering personal. When do you think
these wars will end, Now? Or After?

Alpha-Bait

Paradise is much too small.
Two-legged "Alpha" stands for all—

"Boo-Hag" beside him. A cracked rib
belittles the fall. We zigzag to fecundity.

Confusion in the kitchen-scape. Boo-Hag and Mother
are not to blame for the contraband and thin saucers

of old milk in rancid times. Boo-Hag and Mother are the same.
They know everything concerning pure points and asymmetry.

Boo-Hag and Mother warp space-time, together behind doors.
I'd bait kittens in geomancy with heated points of milk,

then draw the thin lie of a line to connect all four, the kittens
leashed sweet to sour. The lie goes on, something like infinity.

Flints of truth spark the night, the morning milk.
Light the doors, the sour day. The clustered alphabet unleashed

in infinitesimal mews. Word-streams uphill, sleepers having
to unmind each point along the brittle curves

the story that the road retells of what did not happen here…
Connect any two. The road disappears.

The second time I entered I remembered it bigger the first time,
how the milk became the mountains, peak after peak.

And so on until I come to "Zed." I'll say that I saw it
as it really is—time-jagged and emerald,

hallucinating boulders the size of the moon. Travel worn
by orbits on earth I'd never dreamed before.

Duende and The Great Matter of Birth-and-Death

Garcia Lorca called last night (before you get in a twist, he called you
    too.
You didn't pick up). He said, *Disappearance and Death* are real. I
    suggested

he text, but texting's too flat for the poetics of death. Sure, you said,
to no one out loud, ridding yourself of the bitter taste on your tongue.

I feel you quicken, slow drifting away. Turning as you check the
    volume.
Counting the likes, followers, following. Disappearance after
    disappearance.

There's no way to count the air. You think you know death. The Day
    of the Dead
is just ink to you. Garcia Lorca called you last night. Your line was
    dead.

Playing at death in the House of Numb.
Ay! Valiant cruising Internet!
Ay! Needles nattering!

Garcia Lorca is calling from Portland. Pick up!
Pick up! You've disappeared again, strategized
a pretext. Blackout. Death

is instantaneous. Torture, endless. Hunger,
measured. Shit is a scandal of humiliation. Torment
deeper than a half-life is long.

The afternoon is ordinary. You are about to take a next breath, to
    shoot
an email to your publisher that contains your manuscript, *Daily
    Minutia.*

The server is hungry for fresh insights. It drags your text into the nearest
hog-shaped cloud. You have no teeth to speak of.

You ponder atomic particle theory. Trying to manifest reality
bitch-slap the keyboard.

He called from the marshes of Satilla Shores
where there's no reception at all.

He called from Minneapolis, through a busted windpipe
warned you of the mastermind.

He called from Louisville awakened by a battering ram.

He called from Portland choking out the names of vanished people.

He left you a message from Chicago about meeting up in Kansas City.

He called out in Memphis, pleading. He said,

Blossoms fall on the Day of the Dead.
You are a dreaded weed about to be pulled.

Helter Skelter

Night is a stage set for doppelgangers. If not by me
then whom? I should be sleeping but the day's residue
skitters crosswise in my mind.

The snow was coming down hard on my drive to work.
'Helter Skelter' was hammering out of the Beatle's station
intending to wake me. I sang along

through snowy fields clotted with dirty sheep. In the evening
prepping dinner, it popped into my head again. It began
at the sink, singing then dancing 'Helter Skelter' round

the kitchen table. At 2:00 a.m. I was wide awake in my head
still singing 'Helter Skelter' until sunrise—or was 'Helter Skelter'
singing me? Tell me the answer.

At 6:00 a.m. my cell phone 'alarm clock' reminded me—not
every person knows the difference between a madly clamoring bell
they themselves have set, and pervasive radio waves—

one you shut off after ten minutes,
the other never leaves you.

You Are So Confucius: Eastern Alternatives to AA

Keep it simple. When you drink—
drink only enough to unfurl

    curling upward the corners of your lotus petal lips.
Ease does this. Make time for continuous practice.

    On the mild autumn night you were conceived
strong spirits flowed through both your parents.

    Your people are all slurpers of dregs.
The map of their ruin is on your face.

    Do not be harsh with your elders.
Try not to think of kerosene being poured onto ants.

    Think of your palette being formed in the sweetness
of summer grasses and bog ripened juniper berries

    under the aroused sun of the Motherland.
The same rye wind that haunts those lochs and moors

    flows in your veins through mixed blood—
you are the agave cocktail who blooms in Curacao

    just once in every century. Green lime,
bitter-sweet and sour, entwine your DNA

    though your mother did not sample the worm.
Recall Yang—to your guests offer only your finest,

    then seat yourself quietly down the hallway.
When Li drinks, Yang gets drunk.

    The effort you are making is the asteroid shower
that makes for fine weather on other planets—

       —the onion you are eating
       is someone else's waterlily.

The moment we passed through

The moment we passed through
The gate an apple fell—

Great blue waterbird flew off
The brook appeared then swelled

In the dark air of my mind's eye
A whirring sound comprised of wind

Torque and feather's weight—
My whole being ever so slowly lifting

My Mother Insults the Irish for the Last Time

I suppose if you'd gotten a good look at the man, who
(may have) funded The Rising by gab and gadding about
the tavern before she was born, you'd have fallen too.

Years later, there were secret knocks and bathtub gin
in bathroom stalls with nurses during prohibition.

Car crashes in the 30's en route to Mardi-Gras in white linen
and cakewalkers to meet the man, Louis Armstrong.

And chaste, he said, in a wool swimsuit, on-board without
romance to Cuba. The devil beside him wore a slim mustache.

In our suburban kitchen where the liquid amber flowed
he was old enough to be her father. In the cocktail shaker:

the seed pearls of my baby teeth, shaken in long, blue cocktail
hours. My boney bits adrift with Maraschino cherries

that floated like fetuses in cheerless tumblers. I'd extend
my tongue begging a taste of scarlet communion.

Then came the day we quarreled. *Irish?* she said, incredulous.
No, you are not. And I, "Excuse me? Yes. I am." To which,
she snapped, *The only thing they're good for is growing eyebrows!*

Poison for poison, dark soul for soul—
Buried the "O" of antiphon. She dared not recall
the whiter than white, white man—

his black hair glistening, blinding her. A raven's wing
before the sun. Much too good she thought then,
for her soilless base in borrowed chiffon.

Hassam mapped out the world on the café tabletop

among thin glasses
of fresh mint tea
silver server of sugar syrup smiling
the old stone road led to the sea

"the world is this big" said he inscribing
a circle in the crumbs off my breakfast plate
"take me out of here please there is no hiding"
from the world unseen before

everyone has been to this café
small circle in the square of society
the vile Englishman in caftan bays
"I see you've met my little monkey"

everyone has seen this poem gliding
tender daughters slender sons into death-black SUV's
down ancient roads to hotels shining
overlooking the silver sea

Hassam mapped out the world
on the café tabletop among thin glasses
of fresh mint tea
my heart fell dead before*

*"my heart fell dead before" from 'All in green went my love riding.'
e.e. cummings. Public domain.

Rorschach

Gentlemen, grim Fathers,
Here we are together in the sickroom—
Lord Yama of the Underworld
(controlling the controls),
who but belly dancing Bodhisattvas
could grab him by his cherry-red horns?

Tell us of the hindrances. Which is worse—
Doubt (that fraud masquerading as a poet)?
Greed (villeinage to bullets and bombs)?
Anger (too many rounds, so little time)?
Or torpor (not the same as sloth? Don't bother)?

Could you imagine anything as serpentine
as your pliant daughters? Dancing
through the shopping malls? Leaving
there in body bags? Could you, Mothers,
your moody daughters? Sullen

little bitches. Could they become sick?
Of course—Stupidity's contagious.
Lusty monks in monks' cells mistaken
for sublime merely simulate daughters'
irrepressible desire. Together

in the sickroom, she dares not feign
describing the indescribable.

I Think of Them Too Often

I'm thinking of titling my next book of poems, *Kim Kardashian*.
Her entourage and fans all around the world will buy it

thinking there'll be pictures of her ass between the covers
(as if her face to the world), but my agent warned against it.

I used to think of Kim Kardashian, Lady Gaga, and Madonna
often. Intrusive thoughts are diagnostic and may be signs

of mental illness. But not thoughts paid for, inserted by celebrities
to gain entrée to our minds and the prepubescent mons

of girls deformed by imitation for men all over the world.
My heart and mind beg for these images to leave me: Madonna

in a power suit, Madonna mustachioed with pointy boobs. Madonna
platinum blonde. Dark Madonna, *hah!* Madonna polka dotted.
  Madonna

skipping lightly. Madonna pyrotechnic. Madonna with a black eye
spread-legged against the ropes—hardcore porn in places without

laws protecting women. It's clearly time for action—Madonna
with Kalashnikov in camouflage fatigues. Madonna as Cleopatra

carried in by slaves—on a litter of gold of course, Super Bowl Sunday.
Laughable and lame she couldn't care less about sex slavery—

Madonna tripping lightly in kinky boots on the bleachers (she'd never
sit there). Somewhere in the world, imagine, there are people—

who don't crave brands or know the names, Madonna, Kim, Gaga.
The darkening world lights up where thoughts of them don't take—
no need to ward off intrusive thoughts of grotesque celebrity.

Alcohol

My father's days were a clock
calibrated to the second hand
in time for his morning march

to the letterbox. His steps mechanically wound,
the toothed rim of the barrel tight around the mainspring.
The aperture a pinhole set for unquenchable thirst.

Forced to march, locked in return circuit back
to his room, the single shot glass aligned on an imaginary
chute that slid two ways like a game across an old zinc bar

aimed straight into the curve of time—
backward toward oblivion. Next day,
self-wound to the letterbox

to drop one more envelope into the slot. Now,
this dry march of mine, daily up or down,
back or forth to my desk awaiting amends,

saying-writing things with the audacity of a poet,
If you haven't thought of your own death yet, something's wrong.
Wisdom of the dead passed on.

On the Equation of Death

Surely the people are grass.
—Isaiah 40:7

All things bear The Marks of Existence:
Rock   Paper   Scissors. Unsatisfactory—
Terminal—Nonessential.

A Mulberry leaf does not judge me
through stages *wadded with stupidity*—**
faces as bland. If you are still reading

note please first impressions—this
seems a woman's poem: Maybe:
White. Maybe: Old. Maybe: Sexless.

Maybe: Black. Maybe: Asian. Maybe:
Latina. Maybe: LGBQT. All persons
ablaze with ceaseless introspection

in the blazing season. Caterpillars too,
at times take flight. Not as moths or
butterflies. Landing on laps and party dresses.

What happens next is rarely questioned.
Surely grasses shriek beneath the blade.
Ancient, twisted—the pulse surrenders.

** *"wadded with stupidity"* George Eliot

Nothing happened last night

When William Carlos Williams posed this question to his love—
"What happened last night?" then promised to never go to sleep
before you again he wasn't pondering late night TV.

You weren't here. Wool gathering was what
happened last night. The question's whether
or not I've the right to expect you to be here
where nothing's always happening as we both know—
Tendernesses could've been exchanged

instead of spilt milk. Though that's not quite it.
So, let's say *G'-night* for it's hardly worth
the effort it takes to talk about tendernesses
lost or found when the whole kit and caboodle,
the whole shebang persists despite our prayers—

If only we could stop what from happening.

One by one precious nights boil down
not to what but to who. Who will be first?
I simply expect you to be here. How
calm I feel knowing my own desire—
knowing how nearly impossible it will be

to keep from broadcasting my frenzy
when you are not here to tell me what
happened, or I you, nothing
will continue to happen
along with everyone else.

Zero

"What you said, and nothing is the same thing."
—Augustus Saint-Gaudens

Proof hangs upon the hook
the anxious symmetry of zero

I call upon my voice to suckle
in someone else's words against zero

no eyes no ears no nose no tongue
less is so much more than zero

my eyes perceive by breadth of hairs
a slow flame has barely room for zero

oh come now friend surely you can see
differences from eye to eye are zero

flawless moments when we touched
before we turned our backs toward zero

utterance upon utterance ensues
ten-billion words amassing zero

longing in the key of frenzy pools
puddles into lakes with sobs of zeroes

birds exist by virtue of their songs
absence of song's not the same as zero

oh my song there is no song
oh songbirds outflow thrust at zero

La Marseillaise

> *We shall enter the military career*
> *When our elders are no longer there...*
> *Much less keen to survive them*
> *Than to share their coffins.*
>   *—Children's verse, La Marseillaise*

Littleness is power in the face of world terror,
so it warns with beauty *extraordinaire*. To sing inside
the garrison, tread its blood-thick boards, gathering up

power exalted by the song in the openness of vowels
as in; Zaza, Somali, Bajelani. To sing as one voice down
the treacherous scale toward the breaking line of melody

where everyone falters before it drops into the dark plateau.
Then swelling like a multitude, soars to rally us on
with flags, more bombs. A nation's praise of mega-death

in song. Beneath the ever-setting sun someone always cries,
Se lever! Arise! How long we've fed on that treacle, the march.

Wisteria

For Phil and Don Everly

history's nothing if not tangled
vines that govern poet's diatribes

I sit here man-wrangling my dreams
from whose mercurial fits

Mayakovskian clouds drift past
illuminating agitprop striking words

still racing around Moscow
in summer weight gabardine

smoldering in tented trousers
unzipping zipper's envy

some brutish brand of lover's kisses
a whole populace flicking their lips

entangled in the ambrosial stench
of prison vodka cigarettes
            and nasty women

when dreaming I prefer to dream
the dream of luminous harmonies
            dream dream dream
            Dream dream dream dream

fingering cock's combed hair
that in no way ever musses

in dream's entangled vines adoration's
choiceless always *this* but sometimes *that*
            not much of life is real

golden chords purled the day
in and out of alchemies unfettered

dreaming dinner plans from our separate purviews
potato salad made from small potatoes

you shoot me an email saying you'll make the hamburgers
all day we've dreamed the same Cabernet

catastrophe's quotidian in and out of trousers
loomed round us is the sun

sitting like a golden idol atop
Camel's Hump aflame

At first sign of spring

The air has the melancholy smell of snow. Between
the welter of crystalline flakes, blue, bluer, bluest emptiness.

Inside dark PO Boxes strident mosses grip catalog pages,
little beggars baying, *Walk on me!* Lilies don't care

what they weigh on Mars. *Moon Glow* and *Prairie Fire*
don't set their clocks forward or back. They arrive on time.

Round bales lumber in ragged fields, bronzed
sundials about to cast their spell. The wind whips

the flag around. The pole sings to the sun. Brush Hogs
guzzle up state roads commanding the ground awaken.

Fergus barks at the fledgling sky. Church bells sound
a constant Angelus in praise of green and mating design.

Not a single person budges from their homes. Turtles,
cranes, and peepers hold in their eggs like last breath.

Midway

I stand alone within the ranks of strangers
together on the platform of the uptown express
cell phones' obbligato shimmying

somewhere to my right a man answers his
I decide I think to check mine in case I missed a call
I look at my watch

the woman to my left checks hers
I decide I think I'd better write something
about what's happening here

December's *June Bride* lies open
on the lap of the woman seated to my right
no one over forty looks good in white

no one over twenty-one should consider a crown
of seeded foam atop her phantom bride's head
there's not much left in this world for us to do

Who said that?

kindling my desire a blast of energy
the kind a passing radio can't supply with jazzy
news jingle flashes of the war or wild animal sighting

they say the Crazy Tea Lady still lives
on Baldy Mountain
when or if you stop to ask the way

since you've gotten it all wrong
she offers refreshment pointing says
just keep going   straight ahead

Bow To Be Happy

Time is indifferent. The subject as Art is ailing,
appearing, disappearing in the nine times of every now.

We are no more or less than a lantern beetle, careering
along paths of pheromone trails trying not to kill

and be killed. Still wanting is all there is—
a few crumbs amid the golden rings of fraternity.

A makeover and workout with the gals for remedy.
Amassing satisfactions with gummies at the end of the day.

We love to say *at the end of the day,* hoping
what becomes brittle overnight won't break tomorrow.

At the end of the day prayers do not forgive
our afflictions. But what kindness clouds perform—

blowing past those to whom we've had to bow. An ancient
master said *The mountains belong to those who see them.*

And dreams belong to who—settling the dead
at the end of the day—the mind construed of carapace.

A way opens of its own decorum. To see like Borges—
turn the yellow haze of blindness into the gold of tigers.

The True Dragon

Anyone who points to the sky sooner or later
cries out, *Look! Dragon's dancing!* Yielding
in silence anyone can see, symbols, like clouds,

have a shelf life all their own. Sometimes they appear
in a *pas de deux,* or *pas de bourree* before slipping quietly
back into their caves. Other days they stomp so hard

the whole curtain of sky slams down. We turn away
as abruptly, our little flints of sadness hidden. Why not
ponder how they came to colonize the skies—

our imaginations. In times such as ours no one
dances. Show me the mind that thinks of coupling
and squaring off into tidy corners. Breaking the bridge

as you cross over to bow or *dosie-doe.* It's time to realize
our lot—"No, it's not a dragon," I say. "It's a Scottie,
playing," recalling the old magazine advertisement

for Scotch Whiskey and afternoons spent pouring over
the portrait of a perfect family. Mother nestling her five
brilliant puppies. The whole spirited family, upright, alert.

Wet noses shined like dainty black olives as
the iron ball I'd swallowed fanned into flames.
That's how I know the True Dragon. The empty sky.

So Like Things

Is it like those shoes you'd never think
of leaving the house in?
Is it like kid, or glove leather,

soft and supple, then caught
by accident in the rain?
Spotted, stiff, and cracking.

Or is it those chic, black taffeta
pumps, high couture-ecclesiastic
you keep bagged and boxed

beneath the bed, take out to admire
then slip back under? Still,
the day comes sooner than thought,

practically on the heels, with points
of pure marvel—these are no longer new.
Is it really like that?

Karen Morris is a poet and psychoanalyst in private practice in Montpelier, Vermont. She received The Gradiva Award for Poetry (NAAP, 2015) for her full-length collection *CATACLYSM and Other Arrangements* (Three Stones Press, PA). Her poems have appeared in numerous journals including, *NY Quarterly Magazine, Chiron Review, Writers Resist, Plainsongs, SWWIM Every Day, Paterson Literary Review*. She is a volunteer public educator, Ambassador of Hope for Shared Hope International, concerning the impact of the commercial sex industry in global sex trafficking and sex tourism with children. She is a co-founder and transmitted lay teacher at Two Rivers Zen Community, an on-line practice community. *www.tworiverszen.org*